AN ORIGINAL **MAD LIBS** ADVENTURE

YOU'RE ON YOUR Way ___!

by Brian Elling
illustrated by Scott Brooks

Mad Libs
An Imprint of Penguin Random House

MAD LIBS
Penguin Young Readers Group
An Imprint of Penguin Random House LLC

Mad Libs format and text copyright © 2018 by Penguin Random House LLC.
All rights reserved.

Concept created by Roger Price & Leonard Stern

Published by Mad Libs,
an imprint of Penguin Random House LLC,
345 Hudson Street, New York, New York 10014.
Manufactured in China.

ISBN 9781524784980
1 3 5 7 9 10 8 6 4 2

THIS BOOK IS FOR

_____ !

AWESOME PERSON

Hip, hip, hooray!
You're on your way!

_____,
EXCLAMATION
you've come so far!

There was never a doubt
how it would turn out,

because of how

_____ you are!

You wouldn't stop!
You came out on top!

Your lucky _____
NOUN
got you through!

The next course you set
is anyone's bet!

With _____ million
FAVORITE NUMBER
stars above . . .

and only just the one you.

Will you use your amazing

_____

OUTSTANDING PHYSICAL FEATURE

to

_____

VERB

something great?

Will you travel to (the) _____

A PLACE

to be a/an

_____

DREAM OCCUPATION

who's first-rate?

Or will you _____

ADVERB

take aim for the horizon,

knowing the future is

yours to create?

Whatever you choose,
there's no way to lose

when you let your
_____ dreams soar!
ADJECTIVE

But wait a minute!

Hold on to your

_____!
ARTICLE OF CLOTHING

What's the rush?

Not so fast!

Can't the future wait
just a few seconds more?

Because, before you go, there are a few

_____ things
ADJECTIVE
you should know.

There's no one quite as

_____ as you.
ADJECTIVE

And there's no one who can

make people _____

VERB

the way that you do.

Remember that every day!

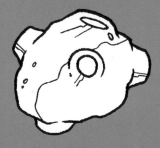

So when you miss the
_____ that you
FAVORITE PLACE
knew best . . .

When the _____
                    FAVORITE FOOD
you're eating doesn't taste
like the rest . . .

When your best efforts to

_____ aren't

VERB

passing the test . . .

And you're feeling

_____ and alone . . .
ADJECTIVE

Take a moment!

Drink a/an _____!

FAVORITE BEVERAGE

Look to the sky to see

how far you've flown.

Remember that the

_____ you knew

CURRENT HOMETOWN

was unfamiliar, too . . .

before you called it home!

And that you never knew
you could _____
VERB
the way that you do . . .

before you started to roam.

And if that's not enough
to give your spirit a boost,
look back to where
you began . . .

so _____ and so small!
ADJECTIVE

And remember that we're all here _____ for you . . .

VERB ENDING IN "ING"

me most of all!

So, with all the mushy-_____ stuff done, there remains only one thing left to say!

SILLY WORD

You're ready!

Get _____!
VERB ENDING IN "ING"

Blast off!

It's time!

Congratulations!

You're on your way!